DIFFERENT & ALIKE

written by Nancy P. McConnell

illustrated by Nancy Duell

©1982 Current, Inc., Colorado Springs, Colorado 80941

What if everyone you knew was exactly like you? What if they had the same color of hair, the same color of eyes and they were just exactly your size? What if they even liked all the same things you liked—the same TV shows, the same games and the same kind of jelly on their peanut butter sandwiches? If people were all this much alike, it would be a pretty boring world!

Luckily, we are not all the same. Some of us are taller than others. Some of us are fat. Some of us are thin. Most of us wish we were something other than what we are at least some of the time! You may have lots of freckles while your brother has none. The boy who sits in front of you in school may be able to wiggle both of his ears while you can't wiggle even one! But you may be able to whistle much better than he can.

Because we are not all exactly alike, we say we are "different." Being different is only another way of being you. You should feel very special when you realize that no one else in the world is exactly like you!

Some differences are greater than others. Your skin may be black, white or yellow—and you notice it's different from someone else's skin. Your family may go to church on Sunday while your neighbor's family goes on Saturday. That's a difference in religion. If you say "y'all" (it rhymes with "ball") and your friend says "you guys," that could mean you come from different parts of the country. Someone who comes from a foreign country would speak even more differently than you!

The important thing to remember about all these differences is that the differences make us who we are. And having different people in the world is what makes it an interesting place to live!

He can wiggle
both of his ears!

3

Some Differences are Called Handicaps

Sometimes you may see or meet someone who is different because they have a handicap (it rhymes with "dandy cap"). A handicap is a difference which makes it harder for that person to do something that is easy for you to do — something like walking, seeing, speaking or hearing. People who are handicapped know they have this difference. They also hope you will feel it is no more important than any of the other things about them which make them different from you. Just like you, they have many likes and dislikes. Just like you, some things are hard for them to do while they can do other things very easily. And just like you, they want to be liked for who they are when ALL their differences are added together.

When we don't know all there is to know about something different, we are sometimes afraid of it. You may be afraid of a person's handicap because you don't understand it, or because it makes that person look or act a strange way. You may even worry that the handicap could be catching! Well, it isn't. It's only different.

All of us know how it feels to be handicapped in some way, if even for a short time. Have you ever been blindfolded to play "Pin the Tail on the Donkey?" If so, you were "blind" for awhile. Have you ever sprained your ankle or broken your leg? If so, you were "crippled" for awhile. Have you ever tried to hear what someone was saying to you from the other side of a glass window but couldn't? Then you were "deaf" for awhile.

The good thing about all the handicaps we just mentioned is that they are temporary. That means that sooner or later they will go away. Some people have handicaps all the time —

differences in how they learn, see, hear or move about that will never go away. Because the handicap will not go away, the person who has it must learn more about it.

First, they must try to understand why they have the handicap. Were they born with it, or was it caused by some accident or illness? What things can they still do? What things will be harder for them to do because of the handicap? Once they know the answers to these questions, then they can begin to learn how to do some of the things their handicap makes it hard for them to do in a new way. After awhile, most handicapped people realize there is still so much for them to learn, experience and feel that having the handicap doesn't really matter so much after all.

You were "blind" for awhile.

Being Deaf

If you were watching television and something suddenly happened to the sound, you would be very upset and frustrated, wouldn't you? Part of the enjoyment of watching your favorite program would be gone, because you would no longer be able to hear what was happening. However, soon you would stop worrying about hearing and you would try to figure out what was happening in other ways. You would watch what the people were doing and the expressions on their faces. Maybe you would even watch their lips to see if you could figure out what they were saying. Deaf people do these things, too.

Being deaf, or unable to hear, can be caused by many things. Like blindness, deafness can be present at birth or can be a result of an illness or accident. Some people are only "hearing impaired" and can be helped to hear better by a small radio-type appliance called a hearing aid. People who are totally deaf need to learn new ways to communicate.

Since deaf people can no longer hear with their ears, they learn to "hear" by using their eyes. With their eyes they can tell what you are saying by "reading" your lips. Talk to your friends by moving your lips without making a sound. Can they understand what you are saying? If so, then they are reading your lips.

If something suddenly
happened to the sound,
you would be very upset!

duell

7

Deaf people also have a special way of using their hands to "talk" to each other. The "manual alphabet" shown here has a hand sign for *every* letter of the alphabet! Notice how some of the signs look very much like the letter they represent.

Using this guide, you can spell anything you want to say with your hands. Practice saying something to a friend.

Because it takes so long to spell out words letter by letter, however, deaf people also use a system of hand signing in which one sign stands for a whole word, phrase or emotion. You "talk" like this every day without even knowing it!

If a player on your school's basketball team scores a winning goal, do you put your hands in your pockets or clap them together? If you are telling your mom you have a stomachache, do you hold your head or your stomach? If you are angry, is your hand clenched in a fist or waving? See, you use sign language, too!

Practice making the signs in this book. Then think about how many other signs you know.

Signing is especially important to people who are deaf from birth as they often have trouble learning to speak. Babies learn to talk by repeating what they hear. That's why it takes a lot of special training to teach a person who has always been deaf to speak.

You use
sign language, too!

I love you.

Thank you

Help you?

Friend

11

In addition to hearing aids, other special tools are used to help people who are hard of hearing or deaf. A special telephone, which includes a keyboard like a typewriter and a computer-type screen, allows one deaf person to send a message to another deaf person over the telephone wires. One person "calls" another by typing the message on the keyboard. A red light on the "phone" on the receiving end begins flashing as the message comes in so the other deaf person knows to look at the screen and read the message.

Dogs have been trained to help deaf people, too. They alert their masters when someone is at the door by touching them in a certain way. They are also trained to react to all kinds of danger, especially fire, in order to protect their masters.

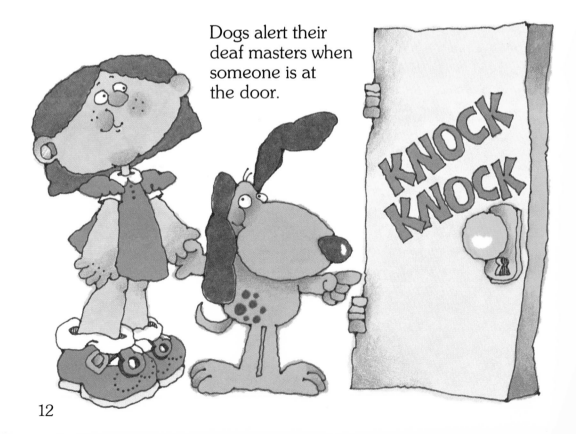

Dogs alert their deaf masters when someone is at the door.

Being Blind

Being totally blind is like always being in the dark, and it is a difference which takes quite a bit of adjustment. While some people are only "partially blind" and can still see shapes and shadows (like being in a camping tent at dawn!), other people can't see anything at all. Remember how we said deaf people learn to "talk" with their hands and "hear" with their eyes? Well, blind people can learn to "see" using their hands and ears.

Being "partially blind" is like being in a tent at dawn.

Have you ever gone to the museum or library where there is a "touch and feel" box? You can stick your hand into this box and feel things—like snakeskin, or deer fur, or bird feathers—that you cannot see. You can't see these things with your eyes, but because you can feel them, you know what they are. You "see" them with your hands.

Even when we are tiny babies we learn about many things by feeling them. Blind people learn to do this all over again. They can even read by feeling!

Babies learn about many things by feeling them.

The special system which was invented to help blind people read is called Braille (it rhymes with "sail"). Books which are printed in Braille have a series of raised dots which stand for certain letters and words . Did you feel the Braille on this page as you were reading? If not, go back and " read " it again with your fingers .

Blind people have other special ways of doing things, too. They listen very carefully. By listening, they know when someone enters the room, or when the cars have stopped at the traffic light and it's safe to cross the street. They also memorize where everything is in their homes so they can move about freely and not bump into any of the furniture. Some blind people have special dogs, called "Seeing Eye™ dogs," who help them by leading them safely from place to place. These dogs actually become the "eyes" of their masters.

Blind people might also carry white canes to help them find their way from one place to another and as a sign to other people that they are blind.

Seeing Eye dogs become the "eyes" of their masters.

Being Deaf and Blind

Some people are doubly handicapped because they are deaf AND blind. This means they can't use their ears to help them "see" or their eyes to help them "hear." Even these people are able to communicate, however.

Many deaf-blind persons "hear" through palm printing or finger spelling. In palm printing, each letter in a word is traced in the palm of the deaf-blind person. Ask someone to write a secret message on your back with their finger. Can you figure out what they are saying? This is how palm printing works.

In finger spelling, a series of finger and knuckle positions for each letter of the alphabet are placed in the cupped hand of another person. Braille is also a big help to the deaf-blind person and, thanks to a new device, a punched tape of Braille can be sent from one person to another and "read" by the person who receives the message.

Ask someone to write
a secret message on your
back with their finger.

Having Learning Disabilities and Speech Disorders

Think about how your mind differs from someone else's. You may be a real whiz kid in math, but just barely pass those weekly spelling tests. Maybe your sister asks you for help with her math homework every night, but always wins the spelling bee! You and your sister are different.

You may have noticed that someone in your class needs more time to learn something new than the rest of the class does. This person may have a handicap called a "learning disability."

People with learning disabilities may look at the word "saw" and actually see the word "was" instead, because some words get turned around backwards in their minds. Or, they may see some letters differently—"nose" may look like "mose" for instance! That's why they have to try extra hard to learn to read. Sometimes they get very frustrated. It's not really helpful to tell a person with a learning disability to hurry up, because they are probably doing the best they can! Special teachers can help these people overcome their handicap in time. It just takes lots of patience.

We all know someone who stutters, lisps, or has other trouble speaking clearly. They may have a "speech or language disorder." By working with a special teacher called a "speech and language therapist," children and adults can often overcome their speech disorders and learn to speak more clearly.

You and your
sister are different.

Being Physically Handicapped

Have you ever stubbed your toe or stepped on a bee when you were barefooted and had to hop all the way home on one foot? Did you ever run in a potato relay with one arm tied behind your back? Then you have some idea how it feels to be physically handicapped.

Physical handicaps are differences which are usually easy to notice. Someone who is physically handicapped may be in a wheelchair, on crutches, have a brace on their leg, or have an arm or leg missing.

People with physical handicaps must learn to be very clever and develop new ways to do the things they used to do more easily. For instance, did you ever think about how a person in a wheelchair would get dressed? Sit in a chair in front of your closet and think about how you would reach your clothes. Soon you would "invent" a tool to help you, wouldn't you?

Luckily, many special tools and many kinds of special equipment have been invented to help people with physical handicaps—including artificial arms, legs, hands and feet!

Look around in your school or the building where you shop or live and see how many things have been changed to help physically handicapped people. Is the drinking fountain lower? Is there a railing in the bathroom? You have probably noticed specially marked parking spaces for handicapped people, too. These spaces are close to the building to make it easier for handicapped people to get in and out. With just a little help and some very simple changes, physically handicapped people can do almost everything you can do.

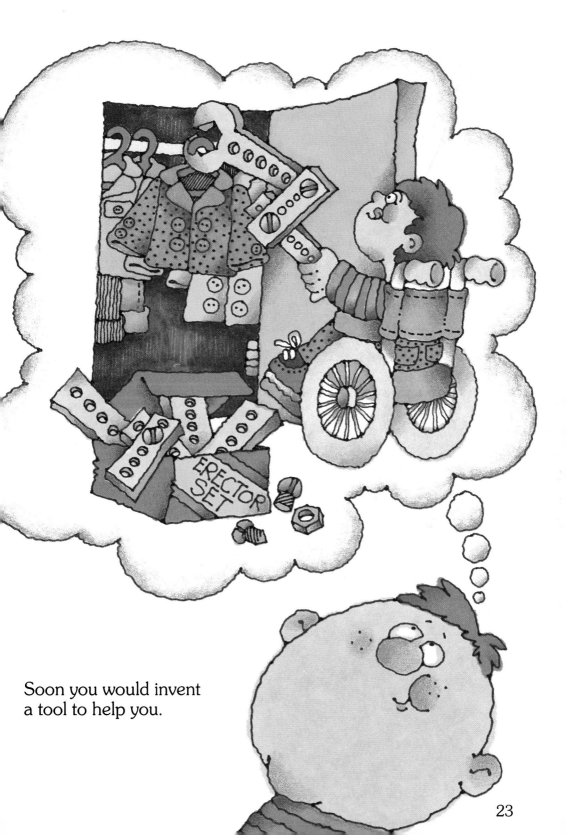

Soon you would invent
a tool to help you.

23

Being Mentally Handicapped

When the differences that exist in someone's mind are great enough to keep that person from learning and growing normally, we say the person with that difference is mentally handicapped. If someone has a serious mental handicap, we say they are "mentally retarded."

There are about six million mentally retarded people living in the United States today. Most of them, about eight out of every ten, are only "mildly retarded" and can learn almost everything you can learn when they receive special instruction. Some of them need to be cared for by other people all their lives.

You need to remember that while mentally retarded people may not be able to do everything you can do, they can do many things. Best of all, they can be loving friends who are grateful for any help you give them!

Helping a Handicapped Person

Remember how we said all people are different, and having a handicap is just one kind of difference? Knowing that is true is the best way to help a handicapped person, but there are other ways, too.

When you are with a deaf person, remember that shouting really won't do any good— it will only make you red in the face and give you a sore throat! Instead, make sure you are looking directly at the deaf person when you talk and you are speaking as clearly as possible. Then it will be easy for the person to read your lips. Use as much sign language as possible, using your hands and your body, even if you don't know the manual alphabet or the official signing system. Remember, some signs are easily understood by everyone!

If you know someone who is blind, remember that being blind is only one difference. A blind person can usually hear perfectly well, so don't ask someone else how blind people feel or what they want to do—ask them! If you are eating dinner with a blind person, tell him or her about the food. It is helpful to ask the person to think of the dinner plate as a clock. Then you can say, "Your meat is at 2:00, your potatoes are at 4:30!"

houting will
nly make you
ed in the face!

It may be helpful for you to guide a blind person, but make sure you ask if they need your help first. Sometimes blind people feel they are being pushed or pulled around like a lawn mower or something! That really doesn't feel very helpful. You can be a "sighted guide" for a blind person by allowing them to hold on to you. They will know when to go and when to stop by feeling your movement.

The best way to help a person with a learning disability or a speech disorder is to be patient. Don't try to do the reading or the speaking for the other person. Of course, it's never helpful to laugh AT a person with a learning disability or any kind of handicap, but it is often helpful to laugh WITH them!

People who have physical handicaps will sometimes need your help to open a door, cross a street, or maybe even to eat or drink. Ask them how you may help, or if your help is needed at all. You don't want to do something for your friend that he or she is proud of being able to do alone. We all know how frustrating that can be!

To be a friend to people who are mentally retarded, encourage them to do their very best at all the things they can do. You can help them find out what they do best by letting them try to do everything you can do!

People who have handicaps
will sometimes need your help.

Most importantly, remember that all handicapped people are like you in more ways than they are different. Just like you, they can do some things better than others. Just like you, they have lots of different feelings. They can feel happy, sad, excited, frustrated, proud, lonely and loved—just like you. After all, we are all alike on the inside.